Collins

11+
Verbal Reasoning

Quick Practice Tests
Ages 10-11

Faisal Nasim

Contents

About this book

Familiarisation with 11+ test-style questions is a critical step in preparing your child for the 11+ selection tests. This book gives children lots of opportunities to test themselves in short, manageable bursts, helping to build confidence and improve the chance of test success.

It contains 55 tests designed to build key English and verbal reasoning skills.

- Each test is designed to be completed within a short amount of time. Frequent, short bursts of revision are found to be more productive than lengthier sessions.

- CEM tests often consist of a series of shorter, time-pressured sections so these practice tests will help your child become accustomed to this style of questioning.

- If your child does not complete any of the tests in the allocated time, they may need further practice in that area.

- We recommend your child uses a pencil to complete the tests, so that they can rub out the answers and try again at a later date if necessary.

- Children will need a pencil and a rubber to complete the tests and some spare paper to write longer answers. They will also need to be able to see a clock/watch and should have a quiet place in which to do the tests.

- Answers to every question are provided at the back of the book, with explanations given where appropriate.

- After completing the tests, children should revisit their weaker areas and attempt to improve their scores and timings for those tests.

Download a free progress chart from our website
collins.co.uk/11plus

Comprehension

Read the passage and answer the questions that follow. In each question, circle the letter next to the correct answer.

EXAMPLE

Anne bought some new slippers yesterday. They are red with pretty little bows at the front.

What colour are Anne's new slippers?
A   Pink
B   Blue
C   Purple
D   Red
E   Brown

The following is an extract from 'Treasure Island' by Robert Louis Stevenson

He was a very silent man by custom. All day he hung round the cove or upon the cliffs with a brass telescope; all evening he sat in a corner of the parlour next the fire and drank rum and water very strong. Mostly he would not speak when spoken to, only look up sudden and fierce and blow through his nose like a fog-horn; and we and the people who came about our house soon learned to let him be. Every day when he came back from his stroll he would ask if any seafaring men had gone by along the road. At first we thought it was the want of company of his own kind that made him ask this question, but at last we began to see he was desirous to avoid them. When a seaman did put up at the "Admiral Benbow" (as now and then some did, making by the coast road for Bristol) he would look in at him through the curtained door before he entered the parlour; and he was always sure to be as silent as a mouse when any such was present. For me, at least, there was no secret about the matter, for I was, in a way, a sharer in his alarms. He had taken me aside one day and promised me a silver fourpenny on the first of every month if I would only keep my "weather-eye open for a seafaring man with one leg" and let him know the moment he appeared. Often enough when the first of the month came round and I applied to him for my wage, he would only blow through his nose at me and stare me down, but before the week was out he was sure to think better of it, bring me my fourpenny piece, and repeat his orders to look out for "the seafaring man with one leg".

How that personage haunted my dreams, I need scarcely tell you. On stormy nights, when the wind shook the four corners of the house, and the surf roared along the cove and up the cliffs, I would see him in a thousand forms, and with a thousand diabolical expressions. Now the leg would be cut off at the knee, now at the hip; now he was a monstrous kind of a creature who had never had but the one leg, and that in the middle of his body. To see him leap and run and pursue me over hedge and ditch was the worst of nightmares. And altogether I paid pretty dear for my monthly fourpenny piece, in the shape of these abominable fancies.

1. What is a similar word to 'custom', as it is used in the passage?
   A   Costume
   B   Superstition
   C   Culture
   D   Habit
   E   Customary

2. What service did the narrator provide for the man?
   A   He served him food and drink
   B   He checked the weather and provided the man with forecasts
   C   He alerted the man when new people stayed at the "Admiral Benbow"
   D   He set an alarm and woke him up in the morning
   E   He kept an eye out for a seafaring man with one leg

3. Which word best describes the man's attitude to any seamen who stayed at the "Admiral Benbow"?
   A   Wary
   B   Frugal
   C   Callous
   D   Grateful
   E   Welcoming

4. How do we know that the man was reluctant to pay the narrator?
   A   He refused to pay the narrator at all
   B   The man was extremely poor
   C   He often refused to pay but then changed his mind later
   D   He hid away when the narrator asked for payment
   E   The man did not think that the narrator was doing a good job

5. What impact did the narrator's job have on him?
   A   It made him angry and bitter
   B   It made him rich and prosperous
   C   It made him weary and tired
   D   It made him happy and lazy
   E   It made him fearful and paranoid

6. What is the meaning of 'abominable fancies'?
   A   Fancy cars
   B   Deadly fairies
   C   Horrendous illusions
   D   Crazy attacks
   E   Brutal devils

Score: .... / 6

Unnecessary Word

You have 6 minutes to complete this test.

You have 6 questions to complete within the time given.

Each of these sentences is shuffled and contains one unnecessary word. Rearrange each sentence correctly and circle the letter above the unnecessary word from the options given.

EXAMPLE

people too at event were there many to the far

A	B	C	D	E
too	many	to	event	far

(Correct sentence: There were far too many people at the event.)

① and not rain cloud the a was was the in there single sky shining sun

A	B	C	D	E
sun	and	rain	cloud	sky

② you job must you want weather not the decide or accept to whether

A	B	C	D	E
weather	decide	whether	to	job

③ roamed land years dinosaurs millions this ago got of through

A	B	C	D	E
land	got	millions	roamed	ago

④ of ran out unruly patience eventually the with student the teacher of

A	B	C	D	E
teacher	ran	of	with	student

⑤ getting dogs to like whilst meat others some swim detest wet

A	B	C	D	E
meat	dogs	others	some	wet

⑥ fit passenger was the by a sudden coughing overcome trains

A	B	C	D	E
coughing	the	by	was	trains

Score: .... / 6

Cloze

In each question, underline the correct word from the three choices provided in bold.

EXAMPLE

There are many different (1) **ways way types** to solve this problem.

Thomas Edison

Thomas Edison was born in Ohio in 1847. An undoubted genius in the (1) **practice practical**

practitioner application of scientific principles, Edison was one of the greatest and most

(2) **producing ineffective productive** inventors of his time. However, his formal schooling was

(3) **extended limited provided** to only three months in Michigan in 1854. For several years

he (4) **laboured masqueraded played** as a newsboy, and it was during this period that he

began to (5) **rejoice recoil suffer** from deafness, which was to increase throughout his life. He

later worked as a telegraph operator in (6) **various viperous vanishing** cities.

Edison's first (7) **inventories inventions intervals** were the transmitter and receiver for the

automatic telegraph, the quadruplex system of (8) **delaying destroying transmitting** four

simultaneous messages, and an (9) **improved maligned grandiose** stock-ticker system.

In 1877 he invented the carbon telephone transmitter (10) **due for as** the Western Union

Telegraph Company. His phonograph was (11) **notorious notable nonexistent** as the first

successful instrument of its (12) **nice generous kind**.

Score: .... / 12

Odd One Out

You have 4 minutes to complete this test.

You have 10 questions to complete within the time given.

In each question, three of the words are related to one another. Circle the letter under the word that is not linked to the other three.

EXAMPLE

bus	car	truck	foot
A	B	C	Ⓓ

(The other three are types of vehicle.)

(1)

puppy	kid	foal	sheep
A	B	C	D

(2)

small	minuscule	average	tiny
A	B	C	D

(3)

indicate	denote	signify	hide
A	B	C	D

(4)

shove	yank	shunt	propel
A	B	C	D

(5)

potato	carrot	turnip	tomato
A	B	C	D

(6)

cry	bellow	weep	yell
A	B	C	D

(7)

captain	wheel	driver	pilot
A	B	C	D

(8)

transparent	evident	opaque	apparent
A	B	C	D

(9)

dissent	submit	comply	defer
A	B	C	D

(10)

articulate	state	eloquent	orate
A	B	C	D

Score: .... / 10

In each question, fill in the missing letters to create an antonym of the word on the left.

EXAMPLE

FULL   E ⬚M⬚ PTY

---

(1) IMMENSE   M ⬚ NU ⬚ E

(2) KING   ⬚ UBJE ⬚ T

(3) BORROWER   L ⬚⬚ DER

(4) SEIZE   R ⬚ LIN ⬚ UIS ⬚

(5) IMPROVE   DE ⬚ ERIO ⬚⬚ TE

(6) MUDDLED   ⬚ UCI ⬚

(7) YIELD   R ⬚ SI ⬚ T

(8) ACQUIT   C ⬚ NVI ⬚ T

(9) ONEROUS   EF ⬚ OR ⬚ LES ⬚

(10) ABOLISH   A ⬚ P ⬚ OVE

Score: .... / 10

9

In each question, three letters have been removed from a word. Use the clue to help you complete each word.

EXAMPLE

Synonym of REPLY **AN** <u>SWE</u> **R**

(1) Synonym of SOCIABLE **GRE** .... **IOUS**

(2) Antonym of ADVERSITY **P** .... **PERITY**

(3) Synonym of VACANT **UNOCCU** .... **D**

(4) Antonym of BLESSED **CUR** ....

(5) Synonym of SUITABLE **APPR** .... **IATE**

(6) Antonym of CLEANED **SOI** ....

(7) Synonym of BAFFLE **MYST** ....

(8) Antonym of MOURN **R** .... **ICE**

(9) Synonym of RARE **UNC** .... **ON**

(10) Antonym of ODIOUS **AGR** .... **BLE**

(11) Synonym of FUTILE **PO** .... **LESS**

(12) Antonym of STARTLE **FORE** .... **N**

(13) Synonym of DECLINE **DEG** .... **RATE**

(14) Synonym of FIDDLE **EMB** .... **LE**

(15) Antonym of CAUTIOUS **C** .... **LESS**

Score: .... / 15

Correct Sentence

You have 6 minutes to complete this test.

You have 12 questions to complete within the time given.

In each question, circle the letter next to the one sentence that contains correct grammar, spelling and punctuation.

EXAMPLE

(A) I gave him two eggs.

B I gave him two of eggs.

C I gave him too eggs.

D I gave him two egg.

(1) A In order for a dog to be comfortable with their owner, it must be treated well.

B In order for dogs to be comfortable with its owner, it must be treated well.

C In order for a dog to be comfortable with their owner, they must be treated well.

D In order for a dog to be comfortable with its owner, it must be treated well.

(2) A The politician objected from the new law.

B The politician objected to the new law.

C The politician objected on the new law.

D The politician objected by the new law.

(3) A My mother gave my friend and I a present.

B My mother gave a present to me and my friend.

C My mother will give I and my friend a present.

D My mother will give a present to me and my friend

(4) A My love of sweets and doughnuts is preventing me from losing weight.

B My love of sweets and doughnuts is preventing me against losing weight.

C My love of sweets and doughnuts are preventing me from losing weight.

D My love of sweets and doughnuts is prevention me from losing weight.

Questions continue on next page

(5) A   Since conserving our planet is vital, everyone should tried to recycle.

     B   Since conserving our planet is vital, it must be recycled.

     C   Since conserving our planet is vital, everyone should try to recycle.

     D   Since conserving our planet is vital, everyone should try to recycling.

(6) A   The engineers worried so much, that they began to lose their hair.

     B   The engineers worried so much, that, they began to lose their hair.

     C   The engineers worried so much that, they began to lose their hair.

     D   The engineers worried so much that they began to lose their hair.

(7) A   Neither boys or girls were allowed into the exhibition.

     B   Neither boys and girls were allowed into the exhibition.

     C   Neither boys nor girls were allowed into the exhibition.

     D   Either boys nor girls were allowed into the exhibition.

(8) A   I am and will study for the next three years.

     B   I am and will be studying for the next three years.

     C   I am studying and will for the next three years.

     D   I am studying and will continue to study for the next three years.

(9) A   Tim likes playing with Rob as much as Gordon

     B   Tim likes playing with Rob like Gordon.

     C   Tim likes playing with Rob as much as with Gordon.

     D   Tim likes playing with Rob just as Gordon.

(10) A   After working at the company for twenty years, Fred's retirement was expected.

     B   After working at the company for twenty years, Fred retired as expected.

     C   After working at the company for twenty years, Fred's retirement was to be expected.

     D   After working at the company for twenty years, Fred's retiring was expected.

(11) A   My cat is allergic by most types of pet food.

     B   My cat is allergic to most types of pet food.

     C   My cat is allergic from most types of pet food.

     D   My cat is allergic against most types of pet food.

(12) A   "Don't go down there!" my brother screamed.

     B   "Don't go down there", my brother screamed.

     C   "Don't go down there" my brother screamed.

     D   "Don't go down there!" My brother screamed.

Score: .... / 12

Complete the Sentence

You have 5 minutes to complete this test.

You have 10 questions to complete within the time given.

In each question, circle the letter next to the word that best completes each sentence.

EXAMPLE

The girl .... home after school.
A   to
Ⓑ   walked
C   prayed
D   bowed
E   ate

① The politician was respected for her ability to be ...., unlike her colleague who was known to be tactless.
A   brutal
B   strange
C   brave
D   diplomatic
E   generous

② Simon frequently arrived late so we reminded him of the importance of being ....
A   indebted
B   punctual
C   savage
D   common
E   late

③ Harry argued that the new law was beneficial as it helped ordinary people to .... money.
A   lose
B   save
C   grow
D   wither
E   pilfer

④ Having been convicted of murder, the criminal pleaded with the judge to be ....
A   polite
B   harsh
C   frugal
D   outrageous
E   lenient

Questions continue on next page

5 Locking the door when you leave the house is the most .... way to avoid being robbed.

   A   pointless
   B   proud
   C   effective
   D   smartest
   E   desperate

6 The zoo animals had adapted well and were .... in their new enclosure.

   A   degenerating
   B   attacking
   C   flourishing
   D   putrefying
   E   weeping

7 The vehicle manufacturer had to .... their new truck as the engine was clearly faulty.

   A   praise
   B   promote
   C   demand
   D   harass
   E   recall

8 The school decided to construct a new building to .... all the new students.

   A   imprison
   B   bully
   C   accommodate
   D   lament
   E   inundate

9 The celebrity hid her face with a shawl so that she would not be ....

   A   recognised
   B   jovial
   C   varied
   D   wandered
   E   allowed

10 The island contains unusual ...., such as rare birds, tigers, beavers and lizards.

   A   insects
   B   peasants
   C   wilderness
   D   wildlife
   E   people

Score: .... / 10

Synonyms

In each question, fill in the missing letters to create a synonym of the word on the left.

EXAMPLE

| NEAR | C L OSE |

(1) FATAL — LET☐☐L

(2) HALT — C☐☐SE

(3) LACK — D☐FICI☐N☐Y

(4) MAGNIFICENT — ☐RAN☐

(5) LIBERTY — FRE☐☐O☐

(6) QUANTITY — ☐M☐UNT

(7) SCOLD — R☐PRIMA☐☐

(8) SUPPRESS — S☐BD☐E

(9) WANE — ☐WI☐DL☐

(10) TEDIOUS — B☐NA☐

Score: .... / 10

Cloze

You have 5 minutes to complete this test.

You have 12 questions to complete within the time given.

Use the words in the table to fill the gaps in the passage. Each word may be used once only.

EXAMPLE

| feather | curl | shimmered | canopy |

The moonlight .... *shimmered* .... on the surface of the hidden lake.

worn	mighty	reluctantly	brink
double	fear	thrust	easily
injury	powerlessness	weak	insults

The Old Lion

A lion, ① .... out from years of ② .... ,

lay on the ground at the ③ .... of death. A boar rushed upon him

and avenged, with a ④ .... of his tusks, a long-remembered

⑤ .... Shortly afterwards, a bull gored the lion with his horns, as if he

were an enemy. When the donkey saw that the once ⑥ .... beast could

be ⑦ .... attacked without any ⑧ .... of

retaliation, he struck the lion with all his might. The ⑨ .... lion said, "I

have ⑩ .... suffered the ⑪ .... of the brave,

but to be compelled to endure such treatment from you is indeed to die a

⑫ .... death."

Score: .... / 12

16

Spelling Mistake

You have 3 minutes to complete this test.

You have 10 questions to complete within the time given.

In each question, circle the letter under the word containing a spelling mistake.

EXAMPLE

spread	smear	scarse	scary	seared
A	B	C	D	E

(1)

heathen	hairy	heather	hallowed	haseten
A	B	C	D	E

(2)

follower	frozen	farcical	fashist	favourable
A	B	C	D	E

(3)

colore	craven	covering	convertible	catastrophe
A	B	C	D	E

(4)

summary	suggestion	summareyes	suffice	subtle
A	B	C	D	E

(5)

grandiose	generos	glazed	gargantuan	gastronomy
A	B	C	D	E

(6)

reversed	rallying	renovaited	reparations	rebellious
A	B	C	D	E

(7)

desparate	desirable	delirious	dormant	drummer
A	B	C	D	E

(8)

abated	abolished	astounded	aggreived	aggressive
A	B	C	D	E

(9)

powdered	powerless	pagoda	pasture	peasent
A	B	C	D	E

(10)

thespian	thaeter	thrilling	thrashed	thinnest
A	B	C	D	E

Score: .... / 10

Change a Letter

You have 4 minutes to complete this test.

You have 12 questions to complete within the time given.

In each question, change one letter in the word in capitals to create a new word that matches the definition provided. Write the new word on the line.

EXAMPLE

BAD	A synonym of 'unhappy'	*SAD*

1. **START**   Clever   ....

2. **HOUSE**   To drench   ....

3. **ALLOY**   To permit   ....

4. **DEFLECT**   To think deeply or carefully   ....

5. **PETROL**   An expedition to keep watch over an area   ....

6. **POWER**   To crouch down in fear   ....

7. **HOLDER**   To shout loudly   ....

8. **ATTACK**   To join or fasten   ....

9. **MERRY**   Compassion or forgiveness   ....

10. **WRETCH**   A sudden violent twist or pull   ....

11. **DEBASE**   To argue about something   ....

12. **DEFER**   To discourage someone from doing something   ....

Score: .... / 12

Synonyms

You have 2 minutes to complete this test.

You have 7 questions to complete within the time given.

In each question, circle the letter above the word that is most similar in meaning to the word given.

EXAMPLE

large

A	B	C	Ⓓ	E
brief	expanse	tiny	huge	lard

(1) tremble

A	B	C	D	E
treasure	tested	still	shiver	humble

(2) urgent

A	B	C	D	E
pressure	urging	petty	critical	jealous

(3) quarrel

A	B	C	D	E
boat	laugh	coal	row	quarry

(4) pacify

A	B	C	D	E
appease	inflame	ocean	intensify	pacific

(5) incapable

A	B	C	D	E
qualified	copious	unable	easy	impressive

(6) ideal

A	B	C	D	E
idea	factual	idealistic	model	deficient

(7) bashful

A	B	C	D	E
bashing	hate	aggressive	humorous	diffident

Score: .... / 7

Fill the Letters

In each question, fill in the missing letters to create a correctly spelled word that matches the definition provided.

EXAMPLE

E L B O W   A joint in the arm

① ☐ DHE ☐ E   To stick to a surface or substance

② C ☐ ☐ X   To persuade someone to do something

③ ☐ EST ☐ TUT ☐   Extremely poor

④ B ☐ SI ☐ GE   To surround and harass

⑤ C ☐ M ☐ EN ☐ E   To begin

⑥ P ☐ ☐ NEE ☐   One of the first to explore a new area

⑦ V ☐ P ☐ UR   A substance diffused in the air

⑧ I ☐ PUD ☐ N ☐   Not showing due respect for another person

⑨ I ☐ ITA ☐ E   To copy

⑩ A ☐ SE ☐ BL ☐   To put together

Score: .... / 10

Test	# Cloze
15	You have 5 minutes to complete this test.
	You have 12 questions to complete within the time given.

For each question, write the correct letter in each box to complete the word.

EXAMPLE

A ra⟦i⟧n⟦b⟧ow is a multicoloured arc that appears in the sky.

Cyclone

Cyclone was a grizzly cub from Alaska, who ① e☐r☐ed his name due to his wild and

② e☐erg☐tic personality. When his mother was fired at, on a ③ ti☐ber☐d hillside

facing Chilkat River, he and his brother ran away as fast as their ④ st☐m☐y little legs could

carry them. When they ⑤ cr☐p☐ back to where they had last seen her, they thought her

asleep; and ⑥ cu☐☐lin☐ up close against her yet warm body they slept peacefully until

morning.

Before the early morning sun had reached their side of the mountains, the two orphans were

⑦ a☐ak☐n☐d by the firm grasp of human hands. ⑧ Va☐iant☐y they bit and

scratched and bawled aloud with rage. However, it was all in ⑨ v☐in as they were eventually

captured and driven away. Cyclone and his brother ⑩ wo☐d☐re☐ what lay ahead for

them. During the long journey, they were fed some fresh salmon, which they ate

⑪ r☐ven☐usl☐. They did not arrive at their ⑫ ☐e☐tina☐ion until nightfall.

Score: .... / 12

21

Rearrange the Words

You have 8 minutes to complete this test.

You have 8 questions to complete within the time given.

In each question, rearrange the words to create a correct sentence and then write it on the line provided.

EXAMPLE

boy his ate dinner the

The boy ate his dinner.

(1) about other cultures to learn travelling is one way

....

(2) all in turned the the flowers sun face garden the to

....

(3) sloping had the a hooked shoulders and man nose

....

(4) before gushed water forest the through tumbling down the the cliff

....

(5) published scientists in the article that many newspaper the criticised was

....

(6) became and the sold rich many salesman charming cars

....

(7) a result in fine may recycle failure to serious punishment more a or

....

(8) contagious spread rapidly the population can diseases through

....

Score: .... / 8

Antonyms

You have 2 minutes to complete this test.

You have 7 questions to complete within the time given.

In each question, circle the letter above the word that is most opposite in meaning to the word given.

happy

A	B	C	D	E
hippy	sad	calm	up	frozen

1. reveal

A	B	C	D	E
revel	allow	revelation	conceal	show

2. frequent

A	B	C	D	E
grace	visit	shallow	forgive	rare

3. fragrant

A	B	C	D	E
putrid	perfume	flower	fragrance	disaster

4. wasteful

A	B	C	D	E
waste	forgetful	frugal	understand	march

5. abundance

A	B	C	D	E
abuse	scarcity	utter	sarcastic	bundle

6. feeble

A	B	C	D	E
deer	weak	water	fist	powerful

7. vast

A	B	C	D	E
vase	expanse	yell	minute	ground

Score: .... / 7

Comprehension

Read the passage and answer the questions that follow. In each question, circle the letter next to the correct answer.

EXAMPLE

Anne bought some new slippers yesterday. They are red with pretty little bows at the front.

What colour are Anne's new slippers?
A   Pink
B   Blue
C   Purple
(D)   Red
E   Brown

The following is an extract from 'The Poisonwood Bible' by Barbara Kingsolver

Imagine a ruin so strange it must never have happened. First, picture the forest. I want you to be its conscience, the eyes in the trees. The trees are columns of slick, brindled bark like muscular animals overgrown beyond all reason. Every space is filled with life: delicate, poisonous frogs war-painted like skeletons, secreting their precious eggs onto dripping leaves. Vines strangling their own kin in the everlasting wrestle for sunlight. The breathing of monkeys. A glide of snake belly on branch. A single-file army of ants biting a mammoth tree into uniform grains and hauling it down to the dark for their ravenous queen. And, in reply, a choir of seedlings arching their necks out of rotted tree stumps, sucking life out of death. This forest eats itself and lives forever.

Away down below now, single file on the path, comes a woman with four girls in tow, all of them in shirtwaist dresses. Seen from above this way they are pale, doomed blossoms, bound to appeal to your sympathies. Be careful. Later on you'll have to decide what sympathy they deserve. The mother especially – watch how she leads them on, pale-eyed, deliberate. Her dark hair is tied in a ragged lace handkerchief, and her curved jawbone is lit with large, false-pearl earrings, as if these headlamps from another world might show the way. The daughters march behind her, four girls compressed in bodies as tight as bowstrings, each one tensed to fire off a woman's heart on a different path to glory or damnation. Even now they resist affinity like cats in a bag: two blondes – the one short and fierce, the other tall and imperious – flanked by matched brunettes like bookends, the forward twin leading hungrily while the rear one sweeps the ground in a rhythmic limp. But gamely enough they climb together over logs of rank decay that have fallen across the path. The mother waves a graceful hand in front of her as she leads the way, parting curtain after curtain of spiders' webs. She appears to be conducting a symphony. Behind them the curtain closes. The spiders return to their killing ways.

At the stream bank she sets out their drear picnic, which is only dense, crumbling bread daubed with crushed peanuts and slices of bitter plantain. After months of modest hunger the children now forget to complain about food. Silently they swallow, shake off the crumbs, and drift downstream for a swim in faster water. The mother is left alone in the cove of enormous trees at the edge of a pool. This place is as familiar to her now as a living room in the house of a life she never bargained for.

1 Where are the events of this passage taking place?

A   In a city
B   In a tundra
C   In a desert
D   In a forest
E   In a tree

2 What literary device is used to describe the frogs?

A   Simile
B   Analogy
C   Alliteration
D   Personification
E   Metaphor

3 What type of word is 'choir', as it is used in the passage?

A   Proper noun
B   Common noun
C   Collective noun
D   Abstract noun
E   Adjective

4 How many human characters are mentioned in the passage?

A   One
B   Two
C   Three
D   Four
E   Five

5 What does the phrase '...they resist affinity like cats in a bag...' mean?

A   They keep to themselves as much as possible
B   They get along well
C   They fight constantly
D   They constantly lose their cat
E   They prevent each other from finishing the food

6 Why did the children forget to complain about the food?

A   They were too tired
B   They were in a rush and wanted to go swimming
C   They had become grudgingly accustomed to it
D   They actually enjoyed the food
E   Their mother distracted their attention

Score: .... / 6

You have 6 minutes to complete this test.

You have 6 questions to complete within the time given.

Each of these sentences is shuffled and contains one unnecessary word. Rearrange each sentence correctly and circle the letter above the unnecessary word from the options given.

EXAMPLE

people too at event were there many to the far

A	B	C	D	E
too	many	to	event	far

(Correct sentence: There were far too many people at the event.)

---

① across cows herd meadow sheep of slowly the wandered lush the

A	B	C	D	E
cows	meadow	sheep	the	lush

② a had been house and in abandoned condition terrible the was in

A	B	C	D	E
house	in	condition	been	was

③ confuse purpose school to of students educate is the

A	B	C	D	E
of	school	confuse	the	is

④ tall reach necks to long their plants toes in giraffes trees use

A	B	C	D	E
necks	to	tall	giraffes	toes

⑤ event attendees graze enjoyed of than the less half the

A	B	C	D	E
event	less	of	graze	half

⑥ refused the enter police dangerous as too was it to the warm ghetto

A	B	C	D	E
refused	enter	dangerous	was	warm

Score: .... / 6

In each question, underline the correct word from the three choices provided in bold.

EXAMPLE

There are many different (1) <u>ways</u> **way** **types** to solve this problem.

Jupiter

The first (1) **record recorded relied** sighting of the planet Jupiter was by the ancient

Babylonians around 700 BC. It is (2) **named entitled heard** after Jupiter, the king of the

Roman gods. Jupiter has the shortest day of the eight planets as it (3) **swings rotates groans**

very quickly, turning on its axis once every 9 hours and 55 minutes. This (4) **lethargic rapid**

languorous rotation causes a flattening effect, which is why it has an oblate (5) **colour**

temperature shape. One orbit of the Sun takes Jupiter 11.86 Earth years. This means

that when (6) **frowned viewed brought** from Earth, the planet appears to (7) **progress**

moving blunder very slowly in the sky. It takes months for it to move from one (8) **gravity**

constellation field to the next.

Jupiter has a (9) **faint feint liquid** ring system around it. These rings are mostly

(10) **comprised consisted contain** of dust clouds that were caused by impactful

(11) **endeavours meetings collisions** with comets and (12) **animals asteroids**

astronomers.

Score: .... / 12

27

Odd One Out

You have 4 minutes to complete this test.

You have 10 questions to complete within the time given.

In each question, three of the words are related to one another. Circle the letter under the word that is not linked to the other three.

EXAMPLE

bus	car	truck	foot
A	B	C	(D)

(The other three are types of vehicle.)

1.
robin	cuckoo	ant	owl
A	B	C	D

2.
width	metre	height	length
A	B	C	D

3.
orbit	comet	asteroid	meteor
A	B	C	D

4.
attack	hunt	grow	fox
A	B	C	D

5.
trained	pretty	feast	slow
A	B	C	D

6.
London	Denmark	Paris	Madrid
A	B	C	D

7.
engineer	teacher	amateur	receptionist
A	B	C	D

8.
bowl	spoon	knife	fork
A	B	C	D

9.
meander	wander	roam	determine
A	B	C	D

10.
shock	accustom	astonish	jolt
A	B	C	D

Score: .... / 10

In each question, fill in the missing letters to create an antonym of the word on the left.

EXAMPLE

FULL   E ☐M PTY

---

1. ENSURE   J☐OP☐RD☐SE

2. BLISS   SA☐NES☐

3. CHEAP   D☐A☐

4. PASSIVE   ☐CT☐VE

5. PLAIN   P☐ET☐Y

6. RESTORE   DA☐AG☐

7. VOID   ☐AL☐D

8. PROLONG   C☐NT☐A☐T

9. PERSIST   CE☐SE

10. CONCLUDE   CO☐☐EN☐E

Score: .... / 10

29

Missing Letters

In each question, three letters have been removed from a word. Use the clue to help you complete each word.

EXAMPLE

Synonym of REPLY   **AN** SWE **R**

(1)	Synonym of CONGREGATE	**ASSE** .... **E**
(2)	Antonym of FABULOUS	**O** .... **NARY**
(3)	Synonym of AGREEABLE	**P** .... **SANT**
(4)	Antonym of ANIMOSITY	**R** .... **ORT**
(5)	Synonym of IMPRUDENT	**RECK** .... **S**
(6)	Antonym of INSERTION	**OMISS** ....
(7)	Synonym of REMARKABLE	**CONSPI** .... **US**
(8)	Antonym of SPITEFUL	**B** .... **VOLENT**
(9)	Synonym of VEHEMENT	**EM** .... **TIC**
(10)	Antonym of OBLIVIOUS	**ATTE** .... **VE**
(11)	Synonym of JUSTIFY	**D** .... **ND**
(12)	Antonym of STERN	**FR** .... **DLY**
(13)	Synonym of RAMBLE	**CHAT** ....
(14)	Synonym of PERFORATION	**R** .... **URE**
(15)	Antonym of AMBLE	**ST** .... **E**

Score: .... / 15

Correct Sentence

You have 6 minutes to complete this test.

You have 12 questions to complete within the time given.

In each question, circle the letter next to the one sentence that contains correct grammar, spelling and punctuation.

EXAMPLE

Ⓐ I gave him two eggs.

B I gave him two of eggs.

C I gave him too eggs.

D I gave him two egg.

---

① **A** The scientist elaborated about his earlier remarks.

 B The scientist elaborated on his earlier remarks.

 C The scientist elaborated from his earlier remarks.

 D The scientist elaborated with his earlier remarks.

② **A** The judge did not believe that the man was telling the truth

 B The judge did not beleive that the man was telling the truth.

 C The judge did not believe that the man was telling of the truth.

 D The judge did not believe that the man was telling the truth.

③ **A** "How long must I wait for?" demanded the angry customer.

 B "How long must I wait for," demanded the angry customer

 C "How long must I wait for?" Demanded the angry customer.

 D "How long must I wait for." demanded the angry customer.

④ **A** The boy didnt want to go to school yesterday.

 B The boy didn't want to go to school yesterday,

 C The boy did'nt want to go to school yesterday.

 D The boy didn't want to go to school yesterday.

Questions continue on next page

5) **A** Theyr'e too many wild animals over there.

B There too many wild animals over there.

C There are too many wild animals over there.

D Theyre too many wild animals over their.

6) **A** Learning to played a musical instrument requires plenty of patience.

B Learning to play a musical instrument requires plenty of patience.

C Learning to play a musical instrument requries plenty of patience.

D Learning to play a musical instrumant requires plenty of patience.

7) **A** The tourists were desperate to visit London and Paris.

B The tourists were desperate to visit London and paris.

C The tourists were desperate to visit london and Paris.

D The tourists were desparate to visit London and Paris.

8) **A** I love to watch documentaries; they're fascinating.

B I love to watch documentaries they're fascinating.

C I love to watch documentaries; their fascinating.

D I love to watch documentaries, they're fascinating.

9) **A** Dave's new neighbour Sally, was very friendly.

B Dave's new neighbour, Sally was very friendly.

C Dave's new neighbour Sally was very friendly.

D Dave's new neighbour, Sally, was very friendly.

10) **A** Omar mistook James about a stranger.

B Omar mistook James as a stranger.

C Omar mistook James for a stranger.

D Omar mistook James by a stranger.

11) **A** Some species of bear hibernate in winter.

B Some speceis of bear hibernate in winter.

C Some species of bare hibernate in winter.

D Some species of bear hibernate in Winter.

12) **A** Peter ate bacon, sausages eggs and toast for breakfast.

B Peter ate bacon, sausages, eggs and toast for breakfast.

C Peter ate bacon and sausages and eggs and toast for breakfast.

D Peter ate bacon sausages eggs and toast for breakfast.

Score: .... / 12

Complete the Sentence

You have 5 minutes to complete this test.

You have 10 questions to complete within the time given.

In each question, circle the letter next to the word that best completes each sentence.

EXAMPLE

The girl .... home after school.

A   to

B   walked

C   prayed

D   bowed

E   ate

---

1   The student did not know the answers so he ....

    A   hugged

    B   guessed

    C   knowledge

    D   positive

    E   freeze

2   The lecture was useless and .... of any helpful information.

    A   full

    B   waste

    C   plenty

    D   devoid

    E   breezing

3   It was .... to drive in winter due to the icy roads.

    A   easy

    B   faster

    C   gross

    D   yonder

    E   difficult

4   Kate's .... departure surprised all of her colleagues.

    A   abrupt

    B   tried

    C   scheduled

    D   power

    E   notified

Questions continue on next page

(5) The essay scored a high mark because it had a .... conclusion.

   A   terrible

   B   nobody

   C   rotund

   D   excellent

   E   logical

(6) Mary had to choose between black .... blue designs.

   A   or

   B   and

   C   additional

   D   but

   E   from

(7) The workers were .... to receive an extra week of holiday.

   A   joy

   B   delighted

   C   conserved

   D   huge

   E   furious

(8) Paul's phobia of snakes explains why he reacted .... when he saw the cobra.

   A   happily

   B   smoothly

   C   badly

   D   calmly

   E   blissfully

(9) Victoria was feeling full so she decided to .... dessert.

   A   missing

   B   add

   C   trace

   D   choose

   E   skip

(10) The scientist thought the experiment was .... so he did not pay much attention to it.

   A   vital

   B   suspension

   C   fascinating

   D   polite

   E   trivial

Score: .... / 10

In each question, fill in the missing letters to create a synonym of the word on the left.

EXAMPLE

NEAR   C [L] OSE

① DECEPTION   F ☐ A ☐ D

② CONCRETE   F ☐ RM

③ SOAKED   SO ☐ ☐ EN

④ APPROPRIATE   ☐ ON ☐ ISCA ☐ E

⑤ PROGRESS   A ☐ VA ☐ CE

⑥ GENUINE   ☐ ☐ THENT ☐ C

⑦ LIBERTY   F ☐ E ☐ DO ☐

⑧ SUSPEND   DI ☐ CON ☐ IN ☐ E

⑨ LINGER   R ☐ MA ☐ N

⑩ EXERTION   EF ☐ OR ☐

Score: .... / 10

Use the words in the table to fill the gaps in the passage. Each word may be used once only.

EXAMPLE

| feather | curl | shimmered | canopy |

The moonlight ....**shimmered**............on the surface of the hidden lake.

poultry	hundred	refuse	gown
pail	fellows	mishaps	imaginary
unison	daughter	moment	money

The Farmer's Daughter

A farmer's ①... was carrying a ②... of

milk from the field to the farmhouse when she began to think, "The ③...

for which this milk will be sold will buy at least three ④... eggs. The

eggs, allowing for all ⑤..., will produce two hundred and fifty chickens.

The chickens will become ready for the market when ⑥... will fetch the

highest price, so that by the end of the year I shall have money enough from my share to buy a new

⑦.. In this dress, I will go to the best Christmas parties, where all the

young ⑧... will propose to me, but I will toss my head and

⑨... every one of them." At this moment she tossed her head in

⑩... with her thoughts. Down fell the milk pail to the ground, and all her

⑪... schemes perished in a ⑫..

Score: .... / 12

Spelling Mistake

You have 3 minutes to complete this test.

You have 10 questions to complete within the time given.

In each question, circle the letter under the word containing a spelling mistake.

EXAMPLE

spread	smear	scarse	scary	seared
A	B	©C	D	E

1

bestow	believe	beseach	bellow	bravery
A	B	C	D	E

2

summary	summery	suggestion	suttle	sagacious
A	B	C	D	E

3

accuze	accustom	accede	aloud	affront
A	B	C	D	E

4

dumb	definiton	dainty	desire	disease
A	B	C	D	E

5

sane	sauce	salvage	severe	sucumb
A	B	C	D	E

6

curb	conniving	callow	contribute	calous
A	B	C	D	E

7

wretched	worrysome	wrangle	wedding	wrist
A	B	C	D	E

8

lasting	languish	labore	lazy	lodging
A	B	C	D	E

9

unisun	undesirable	utmost	union	umbrage
A	B	C	D	E

10

happyness	halo	herd	humongous	hungry
A	B	C	D	E

Score: .... / 10

Change a Letter

You have 4 minutes to complete this test.

You have 12 questions to complete within the time given.

In each question, change one letter in the word in capitals to create a new word that matches the definition provided. Write the new word on the line.

EXAMPLE

BAD	A synonym of 'unhappy'	_SAD_

1. **PLAYER**   A request for help from a god   ....

2. **RUNNING**   A synonym of 'sneaky'   ....

3. **SEVERE**   To feel deep respect or admiration   ....

4. **DRUG**   To pull along forcefully   ....

5. **FOLLOW**   Having an empty space inside   ....

6. **COMMAND**   To praise formally or officially   ....

7. **CROWN**   A large number of people gathered together   ....

8. **ABUSE**   To entertain or please   ....

9. **CRUMBLE**   To complain in a bad-tempered way   ....

10. **MELLOW**   A deep roaring shout   ....

11. **INSURE**   To make certain that something will happen   ....

12. **FAST**   An upright post on a boat that carries the sail   ....

Score: .... / 12

Synonyms

You have 2 minutes to complete this test.

You have 7 questions to complete within the time given.

In each question, circle the letter above the word that is most similar in meaning to the word given.

EXAMPLE

large

A	B	C	Ⓓ	E
brief	expanse	tiny	huge	lard

(1) feeling

A	B	C	D	E
sorrow	happiness	sentiment	frozen	felt

(2) compulsory

A	B	C	D	E
compulsion	optional	command	temporary	mandatory

(3) shallow

A	B	C	D	E
deep	superficial	thin	water	salt

(4) wisdom

A	B	C	D	E
wise	ignorance	intelligence	wizard	old

(5) unanimity

A	B	C	D	E
discord	gravitate	unite	grovel	agreement

(6) patience

A	B	C	D	E
forbearance	patient	sudden	twitch	hospital

(7) kindle

A	B	C	D	E
amazon	behave	crisp	ignite	book

Score: .... / 7

Fill the Letters

In each question, fill in the missing letters to create a correctly spelled word that matches the definition provided.

EXAMPLE

E ☐L☐ B ☐O☐ W   A joint in the arm

① ☐OM☐ANIO☐   A person with whom one spends a lot of time

② R☐BUK☐   To criticise someone

③ G☐A☐ANT☐E   To provide a formal assurance

④ ☐☐ZARD   A danger or risk

⑤ E☐☐AND   A short journey undertaken to deliver something

⑥ C☐N☐E☐PT   Scorn or disdain for something

⑦ C☐NS☐ME   To eat or drink

⑧ IM☐ERS☐   To dip or submerge in liquid

⑨ ☐ROMINE☐☐   Important or famous

⑩ ☐RA☐ME☐T   A small part broken off from an object

Score: .... / 10

In each question, write the correct letter in each box to complete the word.

EXAMPLE

A ra⬚i⬚n⬚b⬚ow is a multicoloured arc that appears in the sky.

Lord Nelson

Lord Nelson was one of the greatest seamen that ever lived. He ①co⬚man⬚e⬚the

British fleet at the battle of Trafalgar, when the combined navies of France and Spain were

②d⬚feat⬚d, and England was saved from a great calamity. He did not

③r⬚⬚emble a famous admiral on board his ship, the *Victory*, that day. He was a small man,

and his clothes were ④s⬚a⬚by. He had lost one arm and one eye in battle; but with the

eye that ⑤r⬚ma⬚ne⬚he could see more than most men could with two, and his brain

was busy ⑥s⬚rat⬚gi⬚ing the course of the impending battle.

Just before it ⑦co⬚menc⬚d, he addressed his loyal crew, ⑧e⬚co⬚ra⬚ing them

with spirited words, which touched their hearts and raised their ⑨s⬚iri⬚s. "On this day,

England expects every man to do his duty" was the final message he ⑩p⬚ocl⬚ime⬚to

them. Every man did his duty nobly that day, though the battle was vicious and ferocious. It was to

be the last conflict of the ⑪co⬚rag⬚ou⬚commander. He was shot in the back as he

⑫st⬚od⬚down the deck with his friend Captain Hardy.

Score: .... / 12

Rearrange the Words

In each question, rearrange the words to create a correct sentence and then write it on the line provided.

EXAMPLE

boy his ate dinner the

The boy ate his dinner.

1. was to minister the electorate his devoted

   ....

2. many report the details were in leaked embarrassing there

   ....

3. the much too under put teachers pressure are being

   ....

4. the its sky spread the soared wings eagle and into

   ....

5. oppose rebuked to the dictator scornfully those that dared him

   ....

6. sudden by intrusion the diners the restaurant shocked were at

   ....

7. a years founded father ago my company seven manufacturing

   ....

8. events was the recall asked night witness the to that of

   ....

Score: .... / 8

Antonyms

You have 2 minutes to complete this test.

You have 7 questions to complete within the time given.

In each question, circle the letter above the word that is most opposite in meaning to the word given.

happy

A	B	C	D	E
hippy	sad	calm	up	frozen

1 ominous

A	B	C	D	E
dangerous	auspicious	evil	omen	neutral

2 industrious

A	B	C	D	E
bee	industry	tools	factory	indolent

3 precise

A	B	C	D	E
sharp	nail	pointed	precision	inaccurate

4 detrimental

A	B	C	D	E
beneficial	joyous	distrust	destroy	fascinating

5 encourage

A	B	C	D	E
applaud	dissuade	persuade	nag	bravery

6 desolate

A	B	C	D	E
despair	fruity	soil	fertile	ferment

7 obliterate

A	B	C	D	E
oblivion	paper	construct	pave	obstruct

Score: .... / 7

Comprehension

Read the passage and answer the questions that follow. In each question, circle the letter next to the correct answer.

EXAMPLE

Anne bought some new slippers yesterday. They are red with pretty little bows at the front.

What colour are Anne's new slippers?

A Pink
B Blue
C Purple
(D) Red
E Brown

The following is an extract from 'To Kill a Mockingbird' by Harper Lee

When he was nearly thirteen, my brother Jem got his arm badly broken at the elbow. When it healed, and Jem's fears of never being able to play football were assuaged, he was seldom self-conscious about his injury. His left arm was somewhat shorter than his right; when he stood or walked, the back of his hand was at right angles to his body, his thumb parallel to his thigh. He couldn't have cared less, so long as he could pass and punt.

When enough years had gone by to enable us to look back on them, we sometimes discussed the events leading to his accident. I maintain that the Ewells started it all, but Jem, who was four years my senior, said it started long before that. He said it began the summer Dill came to us, when Dill first gave us the idea of making Boo Radley come out.

I said if he wanted to take a broad view of the thing, it really began with Andrew Jackson. If General Jackson hadn't run the Creeks up the creek, Simon Finch would never have paddled up the Alabama, and where would we be if he hadn't? We were far too old to settle an argument with a fist-fight, so we consulted Atticus. Our father said we were both right.

Being Southerners, it was a source of shame to some members of the family that we had no recorded ancestors on either side of the Battle of Hastings. All we had was Simon Finch, a fur-trapping apothecary from Cornwall whose piety was exceeded only by his stinginess. In England, Simon was irritated by the persecution of those who called themselves Methodists at the hands of their more liberal brethren, and as Simon called himself a Methodist, he worked his way across the Atlantic to Philadelphia, thence to Jamaica, thence to Mobile, and up the Saint Stephens. Mindful of John Wesley's strictures on the use of many words in buying and selling, Simon made a pile practising medicine, but in this pursuit he was unhappy lest he be tempted into doing what he knew was not for the glory of God, as the putting on of gold and costly apparel. So Simon, having forgotten his teacher's dictum on the possession of human chattels, bought three slaves and with their aid established a homestead on the banks of the Alabama River some forty miles above Saint Stephens. He returned to Saint Stephens only once, to find a wife, and with her established a line that ran high to daughters.

1. Why was Jem rarely self-conscious about his injury?
   A   Because he looked exactly the same when it healed
   B   Because he was told to ignore it
   C   Because he was still able to play football
   D   Because he knew it would improve one day
   E   Because others were too afraid to mock him

2. What is the name of Jem's father?
   A   John Wesley
   B   Atticus
   C   Ewell
   D   Dill
   E   Boo Radley

3. Which word is a synonym for 'stinginess'?
   A   Sadness
   B   Sharpness
   C   Hardness
   D   Happiness
   E   Miserliness

4. Why did Simon leave England?
   A   He was bored and wanted a new challenge
   B   He wanted to escape the bad weather
   C   He felt there was more opportunity to make money abroad
   D   He was facing persecution in England
   E   He found a wife that lived abroad

5. In what field did Simon make a lot of money?
   A   Hunting
   B   Medicine
   C   Slave trading
   D   Building homesteads
   E   Fur-trapping

6. Which of these words is closest in meaning to 'dictum', as it is used in the passage?
   A   Maxim
   B   Accord
   C   Promise
   D   Dictation
   E   Surrender

Score: .... / 6

Each of these sentences is shuffled and contains one unnecessary word. Rearrange each sentence correctly and circle the letter above the unnecessary word from the options given.

EXAMPLE

people too at event were there many to the far

A	B	Ⓒ	D	E
too	many	to	event	far

(Correct sentence: There were far too many people at the event.)

1 decided home return most the soldiers the battle of to after most

A	B	C	D	E
soldiers	most	return	home	battle

2 smartly were dressed cloth children very always the

A	B	C	D	E
cloth	children	always	smartly	dressed

3 at too scene to it the was firefighters arrived late but the

A	B	C	D	E
firefighters	to	at	scene	late

4 costumes actors in tend to limelight the being enjoy theatre

A	B	C	D	E
tend	enjoy	theatre	the	costumes

5 apology disagreement the helped my to resolve grovelling apologise

A	B	C	D	E
apology	grovelling	helped	apologise	resolve

6 and start around finish bakers blame work morning early in lunchtime the

A	B	C	D	E
morning	blame	the	finish	around

Score: .... / 6

In each question, underline the correct word from the three choices provided in bold.

EXAMPLE

There are many different (1) <u>ways</u> **way** **types** to solve this problem.

Vincent Van Gogh

During his lifetime, Van Gogh's work was (1) **consumed** **exhibited** **dressed** in two very

small galleries and two larger ones. Only one of his paintings was sold while he lived. The great

(2) **majority** **majorly** **minority** of the works for which he is remembered were

(3) **promised** **produced** **calibrated** in 29 months of frenzied activity and (4) **illegal** **urban**

intermittent bouts of epileptic seizures and profound (5) **joy** **despair** **laziness** that finally

ended in suicide. In his (6) **fortuitous** **trivial** **grim** struggle, Vincent had one constant (7) **ally**

nemesis **detractor** and support, his younger brother Theo, to whom he wrote revealing and

(8) **extraneously** **tediously** **extraordinarily** beautiful letters detailing his conflicts and

(9) **glamour** **aspirations** **respirations**.

As a youth, Van Gogh worked for a picture dealer, (10) **pleasing** **gracing** **antagonising**

customers until he was sacked. Compulsively humanitarian, he tried to help (11) **preening**

oppressed **comfortable** families but was jeered at by others. His contradictory personality

was rejected by the women he fell in love with and his few friendships usually ended in (12) **bitter**

joyous **harmonious** arguments.

Score: .... / 12

Odd One Out

You have 4 minutes to complete this test.

You have 10 questions to complete within the time given.

In each question, three of the words are related to one another. Circle the letter under the word that is not linked to the other three.

EXAMPLE

bus	car	truck	foot
A	B	C	Ⓓ

(The other three are types of vehicle.)

(1)

kidney	heart	body	liver
A	B	C	D

(2)

feign	attack	pretend	simulate
A	B	C	D

(3)

bungalow	window	apartment	mansion
A	B	C	D

(4)

maroon	mauve	maternal	magenta
A	B	C	D

(5)

savannah	plain	steppe	garden
A	B	C	D

(6)

salmon	seal	herring	kipper
A	B	C	D

(7)

November	August	March	January
A	B	C	D

(8)

cocoa	coffee	lemonade	tea
A	B	C	D

(9)

ignore	applaud	praise	gush
A	B	C	D

(10)

boxer	labrador	beagle	tabby
A	B	C	D

Score: .... / 10

Antonyms

You have 3 minutes to complete this test.

You have 10 questions to complete within the time given.

In each question, fill in the missing letters to create an antonym of the word on the left.

EXAMPLE

FULL   E M PTY

---

(1) STRIFE   H☐RM☐NY

(2) PERMANENT   T☐M☐O☐ARY

(3) CARE   ☐EG☐ECT

(4) ATTRACT   RE☐EL

(5) IMPROVE   D☐MA☐E

(6) GENIAL   ☐OROS☐

(7) PRUDENCE   ☐☐GLI☐ENCE

(8) COMBINE   D☐SP☐RSE

(9) RELEASE   C☐NFI☐E

(10) BLUNT   S☐NS☐TI☐E

Score: .... / 10

Missing Letters

You have 5 minutes to complete this test.

You have 15 questions to complete within the time given.

In each question, three letters have been removed from a word. Use the clue to help you complete each word.

EXAMPLE

Synonym of REPLY   **AN** <u>SWE</u> **R**

---

(1) Synonym of RESIDENCE   **AB** ....

(2) Antonym of EMPLOY   **DI** .... **SS**

(3) Synonym of OBSTINATE   **STU** .... **RN**

(4) Antonym of BROAD   .... **ROW**

(5) Synonym of FAIR   **IMPART** ....

(6) Antonym of PUNCTUAL   **TA** ....

(7) Synonym of GRACIOUS   **C** .... **TEOUS**

(8) Antonym of BANISH   **WEL** .... **E**

(9) Synonym of ANXIOUS   **APP** .... **ENSIVE**

(10) Antonym of DEPOSIT   **WITH** .... **W**

(11) Synonym of WITHER   **D** .... **DLE**

(12) Antonym of SECURE   **PRE** .... **IOUS**

(13) Synonym of HYGIENIC   **SAN** .... **RY**

(14) Synonym of DISCERN   **P** .... **EIVE**

(15) Antonym of NOURISH   **DEP** .... **E**

Score: .... / 15

In each question, circle the letter next to the one sentence that contains correct grammar, spelling and punctuation.

EXAMPLE

Ⓐ   I gave him two eggs.

B   I gave him two of eggs.

C   I gave him too eggs.

D   I gave him two egg.

---

① **A**   Greg was prohibited about making contact with Beth.

B   Greg was prohibited on making contact with Beth.

C   Greg was prohibited with making contact with Beth.

D   Greg was prohibited from making contact with Beth.

② **A**   The Romans created a vast and influential civilisation

B   The romans created a vast and influential civilisation.

C   The Romans created a vast and influential civilisation.

D   The Romans created a vast and influential civilisation

③ **A**   The boy asked, "Where are we going?"

B   The boy asked, "Where are we going."

C   The boy asked. "Where are we going?"

D   The boy asked "Where are we going?"

④ **A**   Sarah paid for the eggs and bread and put them in her bag.

B   Sarah paid for the eggs and bread and put it in her bag.

C   Sarah paid for the eggs and bread and put them in its bag.

D   Sarah payd for the eggs and bread and put them in her bag.

Questions continue on next page

(5)
   A   Their's no way to know if they're telling the truth.

   B   There's no way to know if they're telling the truth.

   C   There's no way to know if there telling the truth.

   D   Theres no way to know if they're telling the truth.

(6)
   A   Two boys put too many bricks on to the table.

   B   Two boys put to many bricks on to the table.

   C   Two boys put to many bricks on too the table.

   D   Too boys put two many bricks on to the table.

(7)
   A   The three boy's balloon flew up in the air.

   B   The three boys balloons flew up in the air.

   C   The three boys' balloon flew up in the air.

   D   The three boy's balloons flew up in the air.

(8)
   A   The elegant girl entered the room graciuosly.

   B   The elegent girl entered the room graciously.

   C   The elegant girl entered the room gracious.

   D   The elegant girl entered the room graciously.

(9)
   A   It's time for the dog to have its injections.

   B   Its time for the dog to have it's injections.

   C   It's time for the dog to have it's injections.

   D   Its time for the dog to have its injections.

(10)
   A   The manager walked down the aisle and inspekted the produce.

   B   The manager walked down the isle and inspected the produce.

   C   The manager walked down the aisle and inspected the produce.

   D   The manager walked down the aisle and inspected the produse.

(11)
   A   "Sat down!" ordered the officer.

   B   "Sit down!" ordered the officer.

   C   "Sits down!" ordered the officer.

   D   "Seated down!" ordered the officer.

(12)
   A   The council decided about following the mayor's advice.

   B   The council decided within following the mayor's advice.

   C   The council decided from following the mayor's advice.

   D   The council decided against following the mayor's advice.

Score: .... / 12

Complete the Sentence

In each question, circle the letter next to the word that best completes each sentence.

EXAMPLE

The girl .... home after school.
A   to
B   walked
C   prayed
D   bowed
E   ate

---

(1) The final scene was boring and so we hoped that they would ....it.
A   include
B   marry
C   perform
D   omit
E   preserve

(2) She has lots of positive character .... such as patience, compassion and honesty.
A   ignorance
B   behaviours
C   flaws
D   people
E   traits

(3) The lecturer made sure she ....the most important lessons from her presentation.
A   ignored
B   pretended
C   polluted
D   bruised
E   emphasised

(4) It was a cold and dreary day and the sky was ....
A   red
B   blue
C   grey
D   green
E   yellow

Questions continue on next page

(5) Dogs have poor sight but an .... sense of smell.

    A   wonderful

    B   terrible

    C   awful

    D   excellent

    E   praiseworthy

(6) Plastic is a very ....material that is used to make lots of different objects.

    A   brittle

    B   versatile

    C   pretentious

    D   focused

    E   stubborn

(7) The manager hoped his star player was only suffering a ....blip in form.

    A   temporary

    B   ignorant

    C   damaging

    D   permanent

    E   colossal

(8) The cunning general outmanoeuvred the opposing army and ....it.

    A   pleased

    B   groaned

    C   jumped

    D   annihilated

    E   welcomed

(9) The actor was ....for attracting scandal and trouble.

    A   eased

    B   cold

    C   commonly

    D   grown

    E   notorious

(10) You must be very ....and be careful to make sure nobody sees the transaction.

    A   flamboyant

    B   discrete

    C   obsolete

    D   discreet

    E   gravitational

Score: .... / 10

Synonyms

In each question, fill in the missing letters to create a synonym of the word on the left.

EXAMPLE

NEAR   C L OSE

(1) ASSUME   S☐PP☐SE

(2) DEAL   B☐RGA☐N

(3) BANKRUPT   I☐SOL☐ENT

(4) GROUNDLESS   BAS☐LES☐

(5) MONOTONOUS   ☐ORI☐G

(6) PREDICTION   ☐OR☐CA☐T

(7) SORDID   FI☐TH☐

(8) UNUSUAL   ☐E☐ULI☐R

(9) CONTEMPTIBLE   ☐ESPICAB☐☐

(10) REFUSE   RU☐BIS☐

Score: .... / 10

Cloze

Use the words in the table to fill the gaps in the passage. Each word may be used once only.

EXAMPLE

| feather | curl | shimmered | canopy |

The moonlight .... *shimmered* .... on the surface of the hidden lake.

entreated	sizeable	panting	profit
single	simple	labour	worth
uncertain	return	produce	present

The Fisherman

One day, a fisherman, who lived on the (**1**) .... of his nets,

caught a (**2**) .... small fish as the result of his day's

(**3**) .... The fish, (**4**) .... convulsively,

(**5**) .... for his life: "Oh sir, what good can I be to you, and how

little am I (**6**) ....? I am not yet grown to my full size. Please spare

my life and (**7**) .... me to the sea. I shall soon become a

(**8**) .... fish fit for the tables of the rich, and then you can catch me

again, and make a handsome (**9**) .... of me." The fisherman replied,

"I should indeed be a very (**10**) .... man if, for the chance of a greater

(**11**) .... profit, I were to forgo my (**12**) ....

certain gain."

Score: .... / 12

Spelling Mistake

In each question, circle the letter under the word containing a spelling mistake.

EXAMPLE

spread	smear	scarse	scary	seared
A	B	C	D	E

(1)

meegre	meander	mastered	measles	mason
A	B	C	D	E

(2)

fasten	foist	flabbergast	fatige	foible
A	B	C	D	E

(3)

overt	ohdour	ostracise	ogre	objection
A	B	C	D	E

(4)

desserted	drone	division	disappear	devastated
A	B	C	D	E

(5)

mercenary	marinor	massive	mellow	mercantile
A	B	C	D	E

(6)

perverted	plume	passionate	plush	plouhging
A	B	C	D	E

(7)

compliment	carress	couples	complement	converted
A	B	C	D	E

(8)

braggart	braized	boisterous	beggar	bane
A	B	C	D	E

(9)

scabbard	saving	sugary	satin	siphen
A	B	C	D	E

(10)

dieluted	delving	donation	disaster	dastardly
A	B	C	D	E

Score: .... / 10

Change a Letter

In each question, change one letter in the word in capitals to create a new word that matches the definition provided. Write the new word on the line.

EXAMPLE

| BAD | A synonym of 'unhappy' | *SAD* |

1. **MESHED** — Reduced to a pulpy mass by crushing ....

2. **HIND** — The tough outer skin of certain fruits ....

3. **FORGET** — Someone who produces fraudulent copies ....

4. **HEAL** — Passion or fervour ....

5. **MONEY** — Sweet fluid made by bees ....

6. **PATENT** — Having great strength ....

7. **GRAB** — Lacking brightness or interest ....

8. **BLEED** — To mix together ....

9. **MORBID** — To refuse to allow something ....

10. **STONE** — To make amends or reparation ....

11. **GRAPE** — To feed on grass ....

12. **CABLE** — A short story conveying a moral ....

Score: .... / 12

Synonyms

In each question, circle the letter above the word that is most similar in meaning to the word given.

EXAMPLE

large

A	B	C	D	E
brief	expanse	tiny	huge	lard

1. inconsistent

A	B	C	D	E
stable	perceive	permit	erratic	error

2. appalling

A	B	C	D	E
delightful	shocking	proud	pail	desired

3. fickle

A	B	C	D	E
upright	frozen	windy	capricious	feeble

4. scintillating

A	B	C	D	E
shingle	boastful	dazzling	dull	saviour

5. rebellion

A	B	C	D	E
insurgence	army	soldier	rebel	dictator

6. barren

A	B	C	D	E
growth	lush	gazed	barrel	sterile

7. humid

A	B	C	D	E
humour	sultry	frigid	forest	heinous

Score: .... / 7

Fill the Letters

You have 4 minutes to complete this test.

You have 10 questions to complete within the time given.

In each question, fill in the missing letters to create a correctly spelled word that matches the definition provided.

EXAMPLE

E☐L☐B☐O☐W | A joint in the arm

① D☐VE☐SIT☐ | A range of different things

② C☐MP☐EHEN☐ | To understand

③ I☐SOL☐NT | Showing a rude and arrogant lack of respect

④ ☐WELL☐NG | A place of residence

⑤ Q☐AIN☐ | Old-fashioned

⑥ ☐UL☐IVA☐E | To grow or maintain

⑦ ☐O☐LT☐Y | Domestic fowl such as chickens, turkey and geese

⑧ H☐RBO☐R | A sheltered port for ships

⑨ ☐OW | An adult female pig

⑩ Q☐ENC☐ | To satisfy one's thirst by drinking

Score: .... / 10

In each question, write the correct letter in each box to complete the word.

EXAMPLE

A ra⬚i⬚n⬚b⬚ow is a multicoloured arc that appears in the sky.

The Trapper

Most mighty hunters can recount multiple ①t⬚ril⬚ing adventures that they personally experienced

with wild beasts; but probably none of them ever went through an experience ②e⬚ual⬚in⬚

that which Arthur Spencer, the famous trapper, suffered in the wilds of Africa. Spencer trapped some of

the finest and ③ra⬚es⬚ beasts ever seen in captivity and so ④e⬚hil⬚ra⬚ing

adventures were everyday occurrences to him. The trapper's life is ⑤i⬚f⬚ni⬚ely more

exciting and dangerous than the hunter's, inasmuch as the ⑥l⬚tt⬚r hunts to kill, while the

trapper hunts to capture, and the risks are not, therefore, ⑦co⬚p⬚ra⬚le.

Spencer's adventure with the 'scavenger of the wilds', as the spotted hyena is ⑧o⬚t⬚n

called, was something so terrible that even he could not recollect it without shuddering. He was

out with his party on an extended trapping expedition and happened to get separated from his

followers. Somewhat ⑨ov⬚r⬚ome by the intense heat and his ⑩fa⬚ig⬚e, he lay

down and fell asleep – about the most dangerous thing a ⑪s⬚lita⬚y traveller in the interior of

Africa can do. Hours later, when the ⑫sc⬚r⬚h⬚ng sun was beginning to settle down in the

west, he was aroused by the sound of laughter not far away…

Score: ………… / 12

In each question, rearrange the words to create a correct sentence and then write it on the line provided.

EXAMPLE

boy his ate dinner the

The boy ate his dinner.

---

(1) believe to they cure researchers soon be able will that cancer

....

(2) been all evidence judgment to it's until important has the reserve examined

....

(3) do must time to next we endeavour better

....

(4) across zones the in disaster play a crucial charities role world

....

(5) the is hurling the vagrant passengers obscenities at

....

(6) fabricated has it's entire he that quite story the likely

....

(7) ingratiate himself employee the manager the with to attempted

....

(8) parents your want get you to attend from you if must permission

....

Score: .... / 8

Antonyms

In each question, circle the letter above the word that is most opposite in meaning to the word given.

EXAMPLE

happy

A	B	C	D	E
hippy	sad	calm	up	frozen

(1) apparent

A	B	C	D	E
appear	ghost	known	obscure	praised

(2) incompetence

A	B	C	D	E
ability	surrender	robber	cane	loss

(3) bore

A	B	C	D	E
drill	boar	tool	excite	pacify

(4) customary

A	B	C	D	E
suppress	exceptional	willing	customs	length

(5) gradually

A	B	C	D	E
happily	gently	agreeably	promisingly	rapidly

(6) disadvantaged

A	B	C	D	E
murdered	hindered	privileged	broken	disabled

(7) eager

A	B	C	D	E
sharp	eagle	elevated	reluctant	keen

Score: .... / 7

Comprehension

Read the passage and answer the questions that follow. In each question, circle the letter next to the correct answer.

EXAMPLE

Anne bought some new slippers yesterday. They are red with pretty little bows at the front. What colour are Anne's new slippers?

A Pink
B Blue
C Purple
D Red
E Brown

The following is an extract from 'Alice's Adventures in Wonderland' by Lewis Carroll

Alice was beginning to get very tired of sitting by her sister on the bank, and of having nothing to do: once or twice she had peeped into the book her sister was reading, but it had no pictures or conversations in it, "and what is the use of a book," thought Alice "without pictures or conversations?"

So she was considering in her own mind (as well as she could, for the hot day made her feel very sleepy and stupid), whether the pleasure of making a daisy-chain would be worth the trouble of getting up and picking the daisies, when suddenly a White Rabbit with pink eyes ran close by her.

There was nothing so very remarkable in that; nor did Alice think it so very much out of the way to hear the Rabbit say to itself, "Oh dear! Oh dear! I shall be late!" (when she thought it over afterwards, it occurred to her that she ought to have wondered at this, but at the time it all seemed quite natural); but when the Rabbit actually took a watch out of its waistcoat-pocket, and looked at it, and then hurried on, Alice started to her feet, for it flashed across her mind that she had never before seen a rabbit with either a waistcoat-pocket, or a watch to take out of it, and burning with curiosity, she ran across the field after it, and fortunately was just in time to see it pop down a large rabbit-hole under the hedge.

In another moment down went Alice after it, never once considering how in the world she was to get out again.

The rabbit-hole went straight on like a tunnel for some way, and then dipped suddenly down, so suddenly that Alice had not a moment to think about stopping herself before she found herself falling down a very deep well.

Either the well was very deep, or she fell very slowly, for she had plenty of time as she went down to look about her and to wonder what was going to happen next. First, she tried to look down and make out what she was coming to, but it was too dark to see anything; then she looked at the sides of the well, and noticed that they were filled with cupboards and book-shelves; here and there she saw maps and pictures hung upon pegs. She took down a jar from one of the shelves as she passed; it was labelled 'ORANGE MARMALADE', but to her great disappointment it was empty: she did not like to drop the jar for fear of killing somebody, so managed to put it into one of the cupboards as she fell past it.

(1) Which adjective best describes how Alice was feeling at the beginning of the passage?
   A   Suspicious
   B   Grumpy
   C   Bored
   D   Nervous
   E   Excited

(2) At what point did Alice stand up?
   A   When she saw the White Rabbit
   B   When the White Rabbit blinked its red eyes
   C   When the White Rabbit took out its watch
   D   When she decided to make a daisy-chain
   E   When the White Rabbit started talking

(3) Which word is an antonym for 'curiosity'?
   A   Enquiry
   B   Indifference
   C   Inquisitiveness
   D   Laziness
   E   Fiery

(4) Which adjective best describes Alice's actions in the fourth paragraph?
   A   Attentive
   B   Disappointed
   C   Heedless
   D   Cautious
   E   Breathless

(5) What did Alice not see on the sides of the well?
   A   Maps
   B   Pictures
   C   A jar
   D   Books
   E   Pegs

(6) Which genre best describes the writing in this passage?
   A   Non-fiction
   B   Historical
   C   Tragedy
   D   Fiction
   E   Romance

Score: .... / 6

Cloze

You have 5 minutes to complete this test.

You have 12 questions to complete within the time given.

In each question, underline the correct word from the three choices provided in bold.

EXAMPLE

There are many different (1) <u>ways</u> **way** **types** to solve this problem.

Heroes

If there had been no real heroes, (1) **imaginary** **accurate** **jealous** ones would have been

created for people cannot (2) **eat** **live** **regard** without them. In order for society to thrive, the

hero is just as (3) **crucial** **pedantic** **prosperous** as the farmer, the sailor, the carpenter and

the doctor. There have been a great many (4) **different** **hazardous** **frantic** kinds of heroes,

for in every age and among every people the hero has (5) **represented** **stood** **encapsulated**

for the qualities that were most admired and (6) **desired** **sought** **praised** after by the bravest

and best; and all ages and peoples have imagined or (7) **produce** **hurdled** **produced** heroes

as (8) **doubtless** **inevitably** **grimace** as they have made ploughs for turning the soil or ships

for sailing through the (9) **earth** **water** **sky** or weapons with which to fight their (10) **allies**

companions **enemies**. If you want to know what the men and women of a country care for

most, you must (11) **relinquish** **study** **interrupt** their heroes for they represent the (12) **idles**

ideals **ideas** and pinnacle of the perceived richest form of life.

Score: .... / 12

Use the words in the table to fill the gaps in the passage. Each word may be used once only.

EXAMPLE

feather	curl	shimmered	canopy

The moonlight ....*shimmered*........... on the surface of the hidden lake.

rose	bundle	ungrateful	admired
tirelessly	strolling	rendered	talons
fallen	which	taking	hazardous

The Peasant and the Eagle

One day, a peasant was (1) .... contentedly through a field when

he found an eagle captured in a trap. He greatly (2) .... the bird

and worked (3) .... to set it free. The eagle did not prove

(4) .... to his deliverer. Later, when he saw the peasant sitting under

a crumbling and (5) .... wall, he flew towards him and snatched a

(6) .... from his head with his (7) .... When

the peasant (8) .... in pursuit, the eagle let the bundle fall again.

(9) .... it up, the man returned to the same place to find that the wall

under (10) .... he had been sitting had (11) ....

to pieces. He marvelled at the service (12) .... to him by the Eagle.

Score: .... / 12

67

Test	# Cloze
55	**You have 5 minutes to complete this test.** **You have 12 questions to complete within the time given.**

In each question, write the correct letter in each box to complete the word.

EXAMPLE

A **ra**⬚ **i** ⬚**n**⬚ **b** ⬚**ow** is a multicoloured arc that appears in the sky.

The Tournament

The scene was ①**r**☐**t**☐**er** romantic. On the verge of a wood near Ashby was an

②**e**☐**te**☐**s**☐**ve** meadow of the finest and most beautiful green turf, surrounded on one

side by the forest, and fringed on the other by ③**sub**☐☐**an**☐**ial** oak trees, some of which

had grown to an immense size. The ground, as if ④☐**ashion**☐**d** on purpose for the martial

display which was intended, sloped gradually down on all sides to a level bottom, which was

⑤**e**☐**clo**☐**ed** for the lists with strong palisades, forming a space of a ⑥**q**☐**ar**☐**er** of

a mile in length, and about half as ⑦**b**☐**oa**☐. The form of the enclosure was an oblong

square, save that the corners were considerably rounded off, in order to afford more

⑧**co**☐☐**eni**☐**nce** for the spectators. The openings for the entry of the combatants

were at the northern and southern ⑨**e**☐**tr**☐**mit**☐**es** of the lists. These were

⑩**a**☐**ces**☐**ibl**☐ by strong wooden gates, each wide enough to admit two horsemen

riding ⑪**a**☐**rea**☐**t**. At each of these portals were stationed two heralds, attended by six

trumpets, as many pursuivants, and a strong body of men-at-arms, for maintaining order, and

⑫**a**☐**ce**☐**tai**☐**ing** the quality of the knights who proposed to engage in this martial game.

Score: .... / 12

Answers

Test 1 Comprehension

Q1 *D*
Habit

Q2 *E*
He kept an eye out for a seafaring man with one leg

Q3 *A*
Wary

Q4 *C*
He often refused to pay but then changed his mind later

Q5 *E*
It made him fearful and paranoid

Q6 *C*
Horrendous illusions

Test 2 Unnecessary Word

Q1 *C rain*
Correct sentence: The sun was shining and there was not a single cloud in the sky. OR There was not a single cloud in the sky and the sun was shining.

Q2 *A weather*
Correct sentence: You must decide whether you want to accept the job or not.

Q3 *B got*
Correct sentence: Dinosaurs roamed through this land millions of years ago.

Q4 *C of*
Correct sentence: The teacher eventually ran out of patience with the unruly student.

Q5 *A meat*
Correct sentence: Some dogs like to swim whilst others detest getting wet. OR Some dogs detest getting wet whilst others like to swim.

Q6 *E trains*
Correct sentence: The passenger was overcome by a sudden coughing fit.

Test 3 Cloze

Q1 *practical*

Q2 *productive*

Q3 *limited*

Q4 *laboured*

Q5 *suffer*

Q6 *various*

Q7 *inventions*

Q8 *transmitting*

Q9 *improved*

Q10 *for*

Q11 *notable*

Q12 *kind*

Test 4 Odd One Out

Q1 *D sheep*
The other three are types of young animal.

Q2 *C average*
The other three are synonyms.

Q3 *D hide*
The other three are synonyms.

Q4 *B yank*
The other three involve a movement of pushing away.

Q5 *D tomato*
The other three grow underground.

Q6 *C weep*
The other three are synonyms.

Q7 *B wheel*
The other three are people controlling a vehicle.

Q8 *C opaque*
The other three are synonyms.

Q9 *A dissent*
The other three are synonyms.

Q10 *C eloquent*
The other three are verbs.

Test 5 Antonyms

Q1 *MINUTE*

Q2 *SUBJECT*

Q3 *LENDER*

Q4 *RELINQUISH*

Q5 *DETERIORATE*

Q6 *LUCID*

Q7 *RESIST*

Q8 *CONVICT*

Q9 *EFFORTLESS*

Q10 *APPROVE*

Test 6 Missing Letters

Q1 GRE**GAR**IOUS
Q2 PRO**S**PERITY
Q3 UNO**CCU**PIED
Q4 CUR**SED**
Q5 APPRO**PRI**ATE
Q6 SOI**LED**
Q7 MYS**TIF**Y
Q8 RE**JO**ICE
Q9 UN**COMM**ON
Q10 AGRE**EAB**LE
Q11 POI**NT**LESS
Q12 FORE**WARN**
Q13 DE**GENE**RATE
Q14 EMB**EZZ**LE
Q15 CARE**LESS**

Test 7 Correct Sentence

Q1 **D**
In order for a dog to be comfortable with its owner, it must be treated well.

Q2 **B**
The politician objected to the new law.

Q3 **B**
My mother gave a present to me and my friend.

Q4 **A**
My love of sweets and doughnuts is preventing me from losing weight.

Q5 **C**
Since conserving our planet is vital, everyone should try to recycle.

Q6 **D**
The engineers worried so much that they began to lose their hair.

Q7 **C**
Neither boys nor girls were allowed into the exhibition.

Q8 **D**
I am studying and will continue to study for the next three years.

Q9 **C**
Tim likes playing with Rob as much as with Gordon.

Q10 **B**
After working at the company for twenty years, Fred retired as expected.

Q11 **B**
My cat is allergic to most types of pet food.

Q12 **A**
"Don't go down there!" my brother screamed.

Test 8 Complete the Sentence

Q1 **D** diplomatic
Q2 **B** punctual
Q3 **B** save
Q4 **E** lenient
Q5 **C** effective
Q6 **C** flourishing
Q7 **E** recall
Q8 **C** accommodate
Q9 **A** recognised
Q10 **D** wildlife

Test 9 Synonyms

Q1 LETHAL
Q2 CEASE
Q3 DEFICIENCY
Q4 GRAND
Q5 FREEDOM
Q6 AMOUNT
Q7 REPRIMAND
Q8 SUBDUE
Q9 DWINDLE
Q10 BANAL

Test 10 Cloze

Q1 worn
Q2 powerlessness
Q3 brink
Q4 thrust
Q5 injury
Q6 mighty
Q7 easily
Q8 fear
Q9 weak
Q10 reluctantly
Q11 insults
Q12 double

Test 11 Spelling Mistake

Q1 **E** *haseten* ➔ *hasten*
Q2 **D** *fashist* ➔ *fascist*
Q3 **A** *colore* ➔ *colour*
Q4 **C** *summareyes* ➔ *summarise*
Q5 **B** *generos* ➔ *generous*
Q6 **C** *renovaited* ➔ *renovated*
Q7 **A** *desparate* ➔ *desperate*
Q8 **D** *aggreived* ➔ *aggrieved*
Q9 **E** *peasent* ➔ *peasant*
Q10 **B** *thaeter* ➔ *theatre*

Test 12 Change a Letter

Q1 SMART
Q2 DOUSE
Q3 ALLOW
Q4 REFLECT
Q5 PATROL
Q6 COWER
Q7 HOLLER
Q8 ATTACH
Q9 MERCY
Q10 WRENCH
Q11 DEBATE
Q12 DETER

Test 13 Synonyms

Q1 **D** shiver
Q2 **D** critical
Q3 **D** row
Q4 **A** appease
Q5 **C** unable
Q6 **D** model
Q7 **E** diffident

Test 14 Fill the Letters

Q1 ADHERE
Q2 COAX
Q3 DESTITUTE
Q4 BESIEGE
Q5 COMMENCE

Q6 PIONEER
Q7 VAPOUR
Q8 IMPUDENT
Q9 IMITATE
Q10 ASSEMBLE

Test 15 Cloze

Q1 earned
Q2 energetic
Q3 timbered
Q4 stumpy
Q5 crept
Q6 cuddling
Q7 awakened
Q8 Valiantly
Q9 vain
Q10 wondered
Q11 ravenously
Q12 destination

Test 16 Rearrange the Words

Q1 Travelling is one way to learn about other cultures.
Q2 All the flowers in the garden turned to face the sun. OR The flowers in the garden all turned to face the sun.
Q3 The man had sloping shoulders and a hooked nose. OR The man had a hooked nose and sloping shoulders.
Q4 The water gushed through the forest before tumbling down the cliff.
Q5 Many scientists criticised the article that was published in the newspaper.
Q6 The charming salesman sold many cars and became rich.
Q7 Failure to recycle may result in a fine or a more serious punishment.
Q8 Contagious diseases can spread rapidly through the population.

Test 17 Antonyms

Q1 **D** conceal
Q2 **E** rare

Test 17 answers continue on next page

Q3   **A**   *putrid*

Q4   **C**   *frugal*

Q5   **B**   *scarcity*

Q6   **E**   *powerful*

Q7   **D**   *minute*

Test 18 Comprehension

Q1   **D**
In a forest

Q2   **A**
Simile

Q3   **C**
Collective noun

Q4   **E**
Five

Q5   **A**
They keep to themselves as much as possible

Q6   **C**
They had become grudgingly accustomed to it

Test 19 Unnecessary Word

Q1   **C**   *sheep*
Correct sentence: The herd of cows slowly wandered across the lush meadow.

Q2   **B**   *in*
Correct sentence: The house had been abandoned and was in a terrible condition.

Q3   **C**   *confuse*
Correct sentence: The purpose of school is to educate students.

Q4   **E**   *toes*
Correct sentence: Giraffes use their long necks to reach plants in tall trees.

Q5   **D**   *graze*
Correct sentence: Less than half of the attendees enjoyed the event.

Q6   **E**   *warm*
Correct sentence: The police refused to enter the ghetto as it was too dangerous.

Test 20 Cloze

Q1   *recorded*

Q2   *named*

Q3   *rotates*

Q4   *rapid*

Q5   *shape*

Q6   *viewed*

Q7   *progress*

Q8   *constellation*

Q9   *faint*

Q10   *comprised*

Q11   *collisions*

Q12   *asteroids*

Test 21 Odd One Out

Q1   **C**   *ant*
The other three are types of bird.

Q2   **B**   *metre*
The other three are types of measurement.

Q3   **A**   *orbit*
The other three are physical objects found in space.

Q4   **D**   *fox*
The other three are verbs.

Q5   **C**   *feast*
The other three are adjectives.

Q6   **B**   *Denmark*
The other three are cities.

Q7   **C**   *amateur*
The other three are professions.

Q8   **A**   *bowl*
The other three are cutlery items.

Q9   **D**   *determine*
The other three are synonyms.

Q10   **B**   *accustom*
The other three are synonyms.

Test 22 Antonyms

Q1   *JEOPARDISE*

Q2   *SADNESS*

Q3   *DEAR*

Q4   *ACTIVE*

Q5   *PRETTY*

Q6   *DAMAGE*

Q7   *VALID*

Q8   *CONTRACT*

Q9   *CEASE*

Q10   *COMMENCE*

Test 23 Missing Letters

Q1 ASSEMBLE

Q2 ORDINARY

Q3 PLEASANT

Q4 RAPPORT

Q5 RECKLESS

Q6 OMISSION

Q7 CONSPICUOUS

Q8 BENEVOLENT

Q9 EMPHATIC

Q10 ATTENTIVE

Q11 DEFEND

Q12 FRIENDLY

Q13 CHATTER

Q14 RUPTURE

Q15 STRIDE

Test 24 Correct Sentence

Q1 **B**

The scientist elaborated on his earlier remarks.

Q2 **D**

The judge did not believe that the man was telling the truth.

Q3 **A**

"How long must I wait for?" demanded the angry customer.

Q4 **D**

The boy didn't want to go to school yesterday.

Q5 **C**

There are too many wild animals over there.

Q6 **B**

Learning to play a musical instrument requires plenty of patience.

Q7 **A**

The tourists were desperate to visit London and Paris.

Q8 **A**

I love to watch documentaries; they're fascinating.

Q9 **D**

Dave's new neighbour, Sally, was very friendly.

Q10 **C**

Omar mistook James for a stranger.

Q11 **A**

Some species of bear hibernate in winter.

Q12 **B**

Peter ate bacon, sausages, eggs and toast for breakfast.

Test 25 Complete the Sentence

Q1 **B** guessed

Q2 **D** devoid

Q3 **E** difficult

Q4 **A** abrupt

Q5 **E** logical

Q6 **B** and

Q7 **B** delighted

Q8 **C** badly

Q9 **E** skip

Q10 **E** trivial

Test 26 Synonyms

Q1 FRAUD

Q2 FIRM

Q3 SODDEN

Q4 CONFISCATE

Q5 ADVANCE

Q6 AUTHENTIC

Q7 FREEDOM

Q8 DISCONTINUE

Q9 REMAIN

Q10 EFFORT

Test 27 Cloze

Q1 daughter

Q2 pail

Q3 money

Q4 hundred

Q5 mishaps

Q6 poultry

Q7 gown

Q8 fellows

Q9 refuse

Q10 unison

Q11 imaginary

Q12 moment

Test 28 Spelling Mistake

Q1 **C** beseach ➔ beseech

Test 28 answers continue on next page

Q2	**D**	*suttle* → *subtle*
Q3	**A**	*accuze* → *accuse*
Q4	**B**	*definiton* → *definition*
Q5	**E**	*sucumb* → *succumb*
Q6	**E**	*calous* → *callous*
Q7	**B**	*worrysome* → *worrisome*
Q8	**C**	*labore* → *labour*
Q9	**A**	*unisun* → *unison*
Q10	**A**	*happyness* → *happiness*

Test 29 Change a Letter

Q1 PRAYER
Q2 CUNNING
Q3 REVERE
Q4 DRAG
Q5 HOLLOW
Q6 COMMEND
Q7 CROWD
Q8 AMUSE
Q9 GRUMBLE
Q10 BELLOW
Q11 ENSURE
Q12 MAST

Test 30 Synonyms

Q1 **C** sentiment
Q2 **E** mandatory
Q3 **B** superficial
Q4 **C** intelligence
Q5 **E** agreement
Q6 **A** forbearance
Q7 **D** ignite

Test 31 Fill the Letters

Q1 COMPANION
Q2 REBUKE
Q3 GUARANTEE
Q4 HAZARD
Q5 ERRAND
Q6 CONTEMPT
Q7 CONSUME
Q8 IMMERSE

Q9 PROMINENT
Q10 FRAGMENT

Test 32 Cloze

Q1 commanded
Q2 defeated
Q3 resemble
Q4 shabby
Q5 remained
Q6 strategising
Q7 commenced
Q8 encouraging
Q9 spirits
Q10 proclaimed
Q11 courageous
Q12 strode

Test 33 Rearrange the Words

Q1 The minister was devoted to his electorate.
Q2 There were many embarrassing details in the leaked report.
Q3 The teachers are being put under too much pressure.
Q4 The eagle spread its wings and soared into the sky.
Q5 The dictator scornfully rebuked those that dared to oppose him.
Q6 Diners at the restaurant were shocked by the sudden intrusion.
Q7 My father founded a manufacturing company seven years ago.
Q8 The witness was asked to recall the events of that night.

Test 34 Antonyms

Q1 **B** auspicious
Q2 **E** indolent
Q3 **E** inaccurate
Q4 **A** beneficial
Q5 **B** dissuade
Q6 **D** fertile
Q7 **C** construct

Test 35 Comprehension

Q1   *C*
Because he was still able to play football

Q2   *B*
Atticus

Q3   *E*
Miserliness

Q4   *D*
He was facing persecution in England

Q5   *B*
Medicine

Q6   *A*
Maxim

Test 36 Unnecessary Word

Q1   *B*   *most*
Correct sentence: Most of the soldiers decided to return home after the battle. OR After the battle most of the soldiers decided to return home.

Q2   *A*   *cloth*
Correct sentence: The children were always very smartly dressed.

Q3   *B*   *to*
Correct sentence: The firefighters arrived at the scene but it was too late.

Q4   *E*   *costumes*
Correct sentence: Theatre actors tend to enjoy being in the limelight.

Q5   *D*   *apologise*
Correct sentence: My grovelling apology helped to resolve the disagreement.

Q6   *B*   *blame*
Correct sentence: Bakers start work early in the morning and finish around lunchtime.

Test 37 Cloze

Q1   exhibited
Q2   majority
Q3   produced
Q4   intermittent
Q5   despair
Q6   grim
Q7   ally
Q8   extraordinarily
Q9   aspirations

Q10   antagonising
Q11   oppressed
Q12   bitter

Test 38 Odd One Out

Q1   *C*   body
The other three are internal organs.

Q2   *B*   attack
The other three are synonyms.

Q3   *B*   window
The other three are types of accommodation.

Q4   *C*   maternal
The other three are colours.

Q5   *D*   garden
The other three are words to describe vast expanses of land.

Q6   *B*   seal
The other three are types of fish.

Q7   *A*   November
The other three are months with 31 days.

Q8   *C*   lemonade
The other three are hot drinks.

Q9   *A*   ignore
The other three are synonyms.

Q10   *D*   tabby
The other three are dog breeds.

Test 39 Antonyms

Q1   HARMONY
Q2   TEMPORARY
Q3   NEGLECT
Q4   REPEL
Q5   DAMAGE
Q6   MOROSE
Q7   NEGLIGENCE
Q8   DISPERSE
Q9   CONFINE
Q10   SENSITIVE

Test 40 Missing Letters

Q1   AB*ODE*
Q2   DIS*MI*SS
Q3   STUBBORN

Test 40 answers continue on next page

75

Q4 **NAR**ROW

Q5 IMPART**IA**L

Q6 TAR**DY**

Q7 **COUR**TEOUS

Q8 WEL**COM**E

Q9 AP**PREH**ENSIVE

Q10 WITH**DRAW**

Q11 D**WIN**DLE

Q12 PRE**CAR**IOUS

Q13 SANI**TAR**Y

Q14 P**ER**CE**IV**E

Q15 DEP**RIV**E

Test 41 Correct Sentence

Q1 **D**

Greg was prohibited from making contact with Beth.

Q2 **C**

The Romans created a vast and influential civilisation.

Q3 **A**

The boy asked, "Where are we going?"

Q4 **A**

Sarah paid for the eggs and bread and put them in her bag.

Q5 **B**

There's no way to know if they're telling the truth.

Q6 **A**

Two boys put too many bricks on to the table.

Q7 **C**

The three boys' balloon flew up in the air.

Q8 **D**

The elegant girl entered the room graciously.

Q9 **A**

It's time for the dog to have its injections.

Q10 **C**

The manager walked down the aisle and inspected the produce.

Q11 **B**

"Sit down!" ordered the officer.

Q12 **D**

The council decided against following the mayor's advice.

Test 42 Complete the Sentence

Q1 **D** omit

Q2 **E** traits

Q3 **E** emphasised

Q4 **C** grey

Q5 **D** excellent

Q6 **B** versatile

Q7 **A** temporary

Q8 **D** annihilated

Q9 **E** notorious

Q10 **D** discreet

Test 43 Synonyms

Q1 SUPPOSE

Q2 BARGAIN

Q3 INSOLVENT

Q4 BASELESS

Q5 BORING

Q6 FORECAST

Q7 FILTHY

Q8 PECULIAR

Q9 DESPICABLE

Q10 RUBBISH

Test 44 Cloze

Q1 produce

Q2 single

Q3 labour

Q4 panting

Q5 entreated

Q6 worth

Q7 return

Q8 sizeable

Q9 profit

Q10 simple

Q11 uncertain

Q12 present

Test 45 Spelling Mistake

Q1 **A** meegre ➜ meagre

Q2 **D** fatige ➜ fatigue

Q3 **B** ohdour ➜ odour

Q4 **A** desserted ➜ deserted

Q5 **B** marinor ➜ mariner

Q6 **E** *plouhging* → *ploughing*

Q7 **B** *carress* → *caress*

Q8 **B** *braized* → *braised*

Q9 **E** *siphen* → *siphon*

Q10 **A** *dieluted* → *diluted*

Test 46 Change a Letter

Q1 MASHED

Q2 RIND

Q3 FORGER

Q4 ZEAL

Q5 HONEY

Q6 POTENT

Q7 DRAB

Q8 BLEND

Q9 FORBID

Q10 ATONE

Q11 GRAZE

Q12 FABLE

Test 47 Synonyms

Q1 **D** *erratic*

Q2 **B** *shocking*

Q3 **D** *capricious*

Q4 **C** *dazzling*

Q5 **A** *insurgence*

Q6 **E** *sterile*

Q7 **B** *sultry*

Test 48 Fill the Letters

Q1 DIVERSITY

Q2 COMPREHEND

Q3 INSOLENT

Q4 DWELLING

Q5 QUAINT

Q6 CULTIVATE

Q7 POULTRY

Q8 HARBOUR

Q9 SOW

Q10 QUENCH

Test 49 Cloze

Q1 *thrilling*

Q2 *equalling*

Q3 *rarest*

Q4 *exhilarating*

Q5 *infinitely*

Q6 *latter*

Q7 *comparable*

Q8 *often*

Q9 *overcome*

Q10 *fatigue*

Q11 *solitary*

Q12 *scorching*

Test 50 Rearrange the Words

Q1 *Researchers believe that they will soon be able to cure cancer.*

Q2 *It's important to reserve judgment until all the evidence has been examined.*

Q3 *We must endeavour to do better next time.*

Q4 *Charities play a crucial role in disaster zones across the world.*

Q5 *The vagrant is hurling obscenities at the passengers.*

Q6 *It's quite likely that he has fabricated the entire story.*

Q7 *The employee attempted to ingratiate himself with the manager.*

Q8 *You must get permission from your parents if you want to attend. OR If you want to attend you must get permission from your parents.*

Test 51 Antonyms

Q1 **D** *obscure*

Q2 **A** *ability*

Q3 **D** *excite*

Q4 **B** *exceptional*

Q5 **E** *rapidly*

Q6 **C** *privileged*

Q7 **D** *reluctant*

Test 52 Comprehension

Q1 C
Bored

Q2 C
When the White Rabbit took out its watch

Q3 B
Indifference

Q4 C
Heedless

Q5 D
Books

Q6 D
Fiction

Test 53 Cloze

Q1 imaginary

Q2 live

Q3 crucial

Q4 different

Q5 stood

Q6 sought

Q7 produced

Q8 inevitably

Q9 water

Q10 enemies

Q11 study

Q12 ideals

Test 54 Cloze

Q1 strolling

Q2 admired

Q3 tirelessly

Q4 ungrateful

Q5 hazardous

Q6 bundle

Q7 talons

Q8 rose

Q9 taking

Q10 which

Q11 fallen

Q12 rendered

Test 55 Cloze

Q1 rather

Q2 extensive

Q3 substantial

Q4 fashioned

Q5 enclosed

Q6 quarter

Q7 broad

Q8 convenience

Q9 extremities

Q10 accessible

Q11 abreast

Q12 ascertaining

Notes

Notes

ACKNOWLEDGEMENTS

The author and publisher are grateful to the copyright holders for permission to use quoted materials and images.

P.24 *The Poisonwood Bible* by Barbara Kingsolver, reproduced by permission of Faber and Faber Ltd; P.44 From *How To Kill A Mockingbird* by Harper Lee, published by William Heinemann. Reprinted by permission of The Random House Group Ltd; P.61 Test 49 adapted from *A Terrible Adventure with Hyenas* by C. Randolph Lichfield.

Every effort has been made to trace copyright holders and obtain their permission for the use of copyright material. The author and publisher will gladly receive information enabling them to rectify any error or omission in subsequent editions. All facts are correct at time of going to press.

Published by Collins

An imprint of HarperCollins*Publishers* Limited
1 London Bridge Street
London SE1 9GF

HarperCollins*Publishers*
Macken House
39/40 Mayor Street Upper
Dublin 1
D01 C9W8
Ireland

ISBN: 9781844198948

First published 2017
This edition published 2020
Previously published as Letts

10 9 8

© HarperCollins*Publishers* Limited 2020

British Library Cataloguing in Publication Data.

A CIP record of this book is available from the British Library.

Author: Faisal Nasim

Commissioning Editor: Michelle I'Anson

Editor and Project Manager: Sonia Dawkins

Cover Design: Sarah Duxbury and Kevin Robbins

Text Design, Layout and Artwork: Q2A Media

Production: Paul Harding

Printed by Ashford Colour Ltd.

MIX
Paper
FSC™ C007454

Please note that Collins is not associated with CEM in any way. This book does not contain any official questions and it is not endorsed by CEM.

Our question types are based on those set by CEM, but we cannot guarantee that your child's actual 11+ exam will contain the same question types or format as this book.